TALKING MATH

CHRISTOPHER DANIELSON

How Many?

A DIFFERENT KIND OF COUNTING BOOK

Charlesbridge

This is a book about **numbers** and **counting,** but it's different from other counting books.

This book **doesn't** tell you what to count.

It **doesn't** start with small numbers and end with big ones.

Instead **you decide** what to count on each page. You have many choices.

The longer you look, the more possibilities you'll notice.

TURN the page to see for yourself.

Look at this picture.

How many do you see?

If you thought, "How many **what** do I see?" then you get the idea.

Maybe you'll **count the shoes**. There are two of those. Or maybe you'll count **pairs of shoes**. There's one of those.

There is one box, but how many **shoelaces**? How many **holes** for the laces to go through? (Those are the eyelets.) How many **ends** on the laces? (Those are the aglets.)

Maybe you'll count the **yellow stitches**, or something completely different.

What other things can you count?

Now how many do you see?

This book is filled with **sets of pictures**. Within each set you'll find many things to count. Some things **change**. Some things **stay the same**. Some things might **surprise** you.

Ready to start counting?

TURN
the page.

How many?

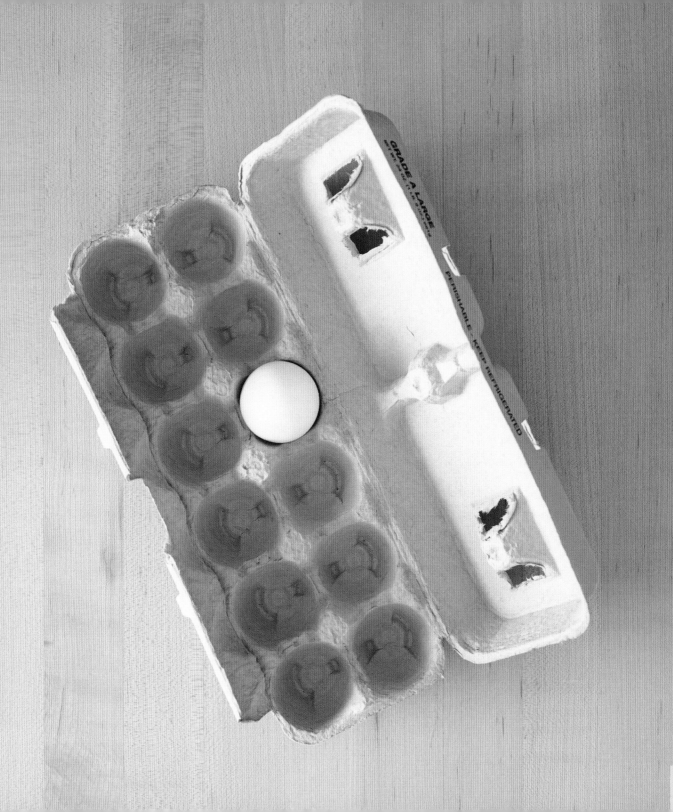

13

How many?

How many?

How many?

How many?

How many?

How many?

How many?

How many?

31

How many?

How many?

Once you've read this book a few times, you might think of new questions to wonder about:

What's the **largest** number in this book?

What's the **smallest** number?

What number is most **surprising**?

What's your **favorite** number? Can you find that many of something on **one** of the pages? Can you find it on **every** page?

What numbers are **missing**?

Your world is full of interesting things. Go count them!

Dear Reader,

Have fun counting. Look closely. Notice new things.

If you think you can't compare apples and oranges (or in this case grapefruits), remember they are both kinds of fruit.

Relationships are important. Two shoes make one pair. Twelve eggs make one dozen. Fifteen avocado halves make one big batch of guacamole.

When you count carefully and clearly state what you're counting, you're doing some great math!

—Christopher